CLIFFORD E.

Rates and Ratios Used in the Income Capitalization Approach

AN APPRAISAL INSTITUTE HANDBOOK

875 North Michigan Avenue
Chicago, Illinois 60611-1980

Acknowledgments

Reviewers: Howard C. Gelbtuch, MAI
Thomas A. Motta, MAI, SRA
John A. Schwartz, MAI
Mark R. Shonberg, MAI

Senior Vice President, Communications: Christopher Bettin
Manager, Book Development: Michael Milgrim, PhD
Editor: Janet Seefeldt
Manager, Design & Production: Julie B. Beich

For Educational Purposes

The material presented in this text has been reviewed by members of the Appraisal Institute, but the opinions and procedures set forth by the author are not necessarily endorsed as the only methodology consistent with proper appraisal practice. While a great deal of care has been taken to provide accurate and current information, neither the Appraisal Institute nor its editors and staff assume responsibility for the accuracy of the data contained herein. Further, the general principles and conclusions presented in this text are subject to local, state and federal laws and regulations, court cases and any revisions of the same. This publication is sold for educational purposes with the understanding that the publisher is not engaged in rendering legal, accounting or any other professional service.

Nondiscrimination Policy

The Appraisal Institute advocates equal opportunity and nondiscrimination in the appraisal profession and conducts its activities without regard to race, color, sex, religion, national origin, or handicap status.

Printed in the U.S.A.

Library of Congress Cataloging-in-Publication Data

Fisher, Clifford E.
Rates and ratios used in the income capitalization approach / Clifford E. Fisher, Jr.
p. cm.
ISBN: 0-922154-23-6
1. Real property—Valuation—Mathematics. 2. Ratio analysis.
I. Title.
HD1387.F542 1995 95-24834

Table of Contents

Foreword

In developing estimates of value real estate appraisers frequently use techniques, tools, and terminology that may mystify or baffle the users of appraisal reports. The use of various rates and ratios in the income capitalization approach, for example, may give rise to confusion or possible misinterpretation on the part of a client or even a reviewer who is unfamiliar with such tools. Appraisers themselves may question the applicability of a specific rate in a given appraisal assignment.

To address these situations, the Appraisal Institute is pleased to publish *Rates and Ratios Used in the Income Capitalization Approach*. Clifford E. Fisher Jr. has provided a handy and unique reference source both for appraisers and reviewers as well as for anyone whose job involves the interpretation of appraisal reports into action plans for real estate development. With this handbook appraisers and others can look up a specific rate or ratio, much as one would look up a word in a dictionary, and get a thumbnail sketch of the function of the rate along with cautions for its application.

Rates and Ratios is the second in a series of handbooks published by the Appraisal Institute on specialized topics. It continues the Appraisal Institute's long tradition of serving the field through an extensive publications program.

Richard C. Sorenson, MAI
1995 President
Appraisal Institute

About the Author

Clifford E. Fisher Jr., MAI, has been a real estate appraiser and consultant since 1970 and an active member of the Appraisal Institute since 1977. He is the owner of Fisher Realty Services in Daytona Beach, Florida. Mr. Fisher holds a degree in education (with a major in mathematics) from the University of Florida. He has taught numerous Appraisal Institute courses and seminars and has played an active role in developing its curriculum and body of knowledge. He has also served on many of its national committees, including its Executive Committee. He has chaired its national Education Committee, Finance Committee, and General Appraiser Board. Other Appraisal Institute activities have included serving as a member of the Comprehensive Examination Subcommittee and Master's Degree Task Force.

Readers of this text may be interested in the following related books from the Appraisal Institute: The Appraisal of Real Estate, *tenth edition*; The Dictionary of Real Estate Appraisal, *third edition*; AIREA Financial Tables; The Appraiser's Workbook *and* Capitalization Theory and Techniques: Study Guide.

For a catalog of Appraisal Institute publications, contact the Communications Department of the Appraisal Institute, 875 N. *Michigan Avenue, Ste.* 2400, *Chicago*, IL 60611-1980.

Introduction

This handbook is a compilation of information regarding the rates and ratios used in the income capitalization approach as currently presented in the Appraisal Institute's educational curriculum. The presentation of some of the material, however, may vary slightly as various nuances are explored that are only implicit in the course or seminar offerings. This is not a textbook in income capitalization. Rather, it assumes that readers are involved in appraisal work (performance or review) and understand the procedures used in income property analysis.

Many times in the preparation or review of an appraisal report a question is raised regarding the magnitude of a rate or a ratio with respect to other numbers presented. Appraisers must be able to identify and avoid contradictions and inconsistencies that could destroy the credibility of their conclusions. Reviewers must not only be able to identify contradictions and inconsistencies, but also have a source of information to accept an infrequently used technique that is appropriate with the available data.

For example, lenders use risk aversion tools (loan-to-value ratios and debt coverage ratios) to reduce their risk below that of a non-leveraged owner. As a result the lender's yield (Y_M) is virtually always less than the property's yield (Y_O). The selection of a property discount rate (Y_O) that is less than or equal to prevailing interest rates for a particular type of property would be an apparent error. The competent appraiser, therefore, will either correct the mistake or, if the market clearly supports that relationship, offer the reader of the appraisal report a convincing explanation. Either of the above will be beneficial to a review appraiser.

To facilitate its use, this handbook is laid out in four parts. Part 1 introduces the necessary background information to support the use and understanding of the handbook. Part 2 provides individual descriptions and explanations of the rates and ratios frequently used in the income capitalization approach. Each rate and ratio is presented with its common name(s), symbol, definition, description, how it is obtained from the market, and its relationship to other rates and ratios. Each concludes with appropriate cautions to avoid misuse.

Part 3 offers a series of examples which illustrate various extraction techniques and point up important and/or frequently misunderstood aspects of the rates and ratios described in Part 2. Questions about the extraction or use of a rate are clarified for the appraiser or review appraiser in this part of the handbook.

Part 4 provides some additional examples, focusing on several legitimate but non-traditional yield capitalization techniques that are likely to become more common in appraisal reports. These topics are extensions or expansions of techniques that have been in appraisal curricula for years. Both the practicing appraiser and the review appraiser would be well served to know these techniques exist and to understand their use.

Users of this handbook should thoroughly read Part 1, which lays the groundwork necessary to understand and use this handbook efficiently, and familiarize themselves with Parts 2, 3, and 4. By doing this, the handbook will be immediately useful to both the author of an appraisal report and to the review appraiser. Experience has shown that not all participants in the client/appraiser relationship completely understand all of the income analysis tools available to the appraiser. Too often, a method or technique is misused, or even worse, an appropriate method or technique is deemed invalid because of lack of knowledge. This handbook was written to prevent these types of scenario from occurring.

The author wishes to extend his personal gratitude and appreciation to Sheila Crowell for her assistance in reviewing and commenting on the original manuscript of *Rates and Ratios*.

PART ONE

Overview of Rates and Ratios

Definitions and symbols are necessary to properly communicate ideas and concepts. Categories, descriptions, and relationships of rates and ratios will serve as the basis for the individual rate/ratio discussions in Part 2 and examples in Parts 3 and 4.

DEFINITIONS

Rate and *ratio* are defined[1] as follows:

> **Rate:** 1) the amount, degree, etc., of anything in relation to units of something else, e.g., the rate of pay per month, rate of speed per hour; 2) a fixed ratio; proportion.
>
> **Ratio:** 1) a fixed relation in degree, number, etc., between two similar things; proportion; 2) the quotient of one quantity divided by another of the same kind, usually expressed as a fraction.

It can be seen from these definitions that a rate and a ratio are quite similar. Both definitions include the word "proportion" and both state or imply that a fraction is involved, either common or decimal. The only significant difference appears to be the implication that a ratio compares two numbers of the same kind of units (e.g., distance/distance, time/time, dollars/dollars) while a rate can (but is not required to) compare numbers representing different units (e.g., distance/time, dollars/time). In real estate appraisal, the rates and ratios used almost always compare numbers that represent the same units. Whether something is called a rate or a ratio appears to have been decided by the originators of the concept and accepted thereafter by convention.

CATEGORIES OF RATES AND RATIOS

The rates and ratios used by appraisers tend to fall into three categories:

1. *Webster's New World Dictionary*, Third College Edition.

Capitalization rate: A fraction used to express the relationship that exists between the income and value of something capable of generating income and having value.

Yield rate: A rate of return on some amount invested. Also referred to as an interest rate, risk rate, internal rate of return, discount rate, etc.

Ratio: In appraising, a comparative term used to describe the magnitude of one number with respect to another, e.g., loan to value, expense to gross income, land to building.

SYMBOLS

Circa 1980, the appraisal profession adopted a system of symbols for capitalization rates and yield rates. Under this system, all capitalization rates are identified by the capital letter R and all yield rates are identified by the capital letter Y. Subscripts, also capital letters, are then used to further identify the kind of capitalization or yield rate that is being referred to, e.g., R_L is the symbol for a land capitalization rate. This system of symbols significantly aids in the written communication of concepts.

Ratios, on the other hand, do not enjoy a simple and clearly identifiable system of symbols. The reader, therefore, can expect more variance in the symbols for ratios in the various writings regarding real estate analysis. The most common symbols used by the Appraisal Institute are included in this handbook.

COMMON RATES

The two categories of rates noted above (capitalization and yield) are the result of the differing ways real estate is analyzed for various purposes, including appraisal. As far as rates are concerned, this handbook is based on the following breakdown:

The whole property: Overall (property) capitalization rates (R_O) and property yield rates (Y_O) are used when analyzing a property on a "whole" basis.

Physical components: For appraisal purposes, a property is sometimes analyzed by its physical parts, land and building. The rates associated with the physical components include the land capitalization rate (R_L), building capitalization rate (R_B), land yield rate (Y_L), and building yield rate (Y_B). Other physical components are possible, but not commonly used, e.g., a separate rate for site improvements.

Financial components: The financial components typically include the mortgage and equity interests. The rates associated with the financial components include the mortgage capitalization rate (R_M), equity capitalization rate (R_E), mortgage yield rate (Y_M), and equity yield rate (Y_E). Again, we are not limited to two components as the analysis may include more than one mortgage.

Legal components: The legal components typically include the interests created by a lease. In the simplest situation, a single lease creates a leased fee position and a leasehold position. The leasehold position may, in turn, lease all or part to another, creating a subleasehold position and a sandwich position. The new subleasehold position might do the same, creating yet another position. For the purposes of this handbook, the leased fee position will be discussed in terms of a capitalization rate (R_{LF}) and a yield rate (Y_{LF}) while the leasehold position will be discussed in two ways as follows: 1) as a single entity having a capitalization rate (R_{LH}) and a yield rate (Y_{LH}); and 2) as a multiple entity subdivided into one or more sandwich positions and a subleasehold position. The capitalization rates, therefore, are R_{SAND1}, R_{SAND2}, ... R_{SANDn}, and R_{SLH}, and the yield rates are Y_{SAND1}, Y_{SAND2}, ... Y_{SANDn}, and Y_{SLH}.

Economic components: By comparison, separate analysis of the economic components is relatively new in the appraisal field. Such analysis views the property in terms of types of future benefits, namely cash flow from operations (NOI, or I_O)[2] and cash flow from reversion. Yield rates, rather than capitalization rates, are normally used in this analysis and include Y_{INC} and Y_{REV}.

In addition to the rates noted above, a discussion of a terminal capitalization rate (R_N) and its use is included in Part 2.

COMMON RATIOS

Ratios used by appraisers include:

Loan-to-value ratio (M)
Debt coverage ratio (DCR)
Land-to-property value ratio (L)
Building-to-property value ratio (B)
Operating expense ratio (OER)
Net income ratio (NIR)

These ratios will be discussed in more detail in Part 2.

2. NOI and I_O are synonymous; they are both used to indicate the net operating income to the whole property.

USEFUL RELATIONSHIPS

The brief discussion of the following relationships will help the reader understand the individual discussions of the rates and ratios in Part 2. These relationships will be used to describe the typical comparative relationships between various rates and ratios (Part 2) and serve as the basis for market extraction techniques shown by example in Part 3.

IRV: This is the basic relationship that relates an income, a capitalization rate, and value. It is useful in three forms:

$I = R \times V$

$R = I/V$

$V = I/R.$

$R = Y - \Delta \times a$: This is one of the most important relationships to an appraiser. Not only does it demonstrate the relative magnitudes of capitalization rates (R) and yield rates (Y) under various market conditions, but it is also useful in estimating one of these rates when the other is known. It is also useful in three forms:

1) $R = Y - \Delta \times 1/S_{\overline{n}|}$ whenever income is expected to be level.
2) $R = Y - \Delta \times 1/n$ whenever income is expected to change by a constant amount.
3) $R = Y - CR$ whenever income is expected to change by a constant ratio. CR is the compound rate of change for both income and value.

"Ellwood": $R_O = \dfrac{Y_E - M(Y_E + P \times 1/S_{\overline{n}|} - R_M) - \Delta_O \times 1/S_{\overline{n}|}}{\text{income stabilization factor}}$

$Y_L = Y_O = Y_B$: This relationship illustrates the usual relative risks of the physical components of a property. Investors rarely assign a different risk rate to land and building.

$Y_M < Y_O < Y_E$: This relationship illustrates the usual relative risks of the financial components of a property. The lender uses risk aversion tools (loan-to-value ratios and debt coverage ratios) to reduce his/her risk below that of the property (or non-leveraged owner). The result is that the equity position's risk (Y_E) is greater than either Y_O or Y_M. This is an example of positive leverage based on *yields*. Negative leverage ($Y_M > Y_O > Y_E$) or neutral leverage ($Y_M = Y_O = Y_E$) is possible but occurs very infrequently as it is not generally acceptable to the prudent investor.

$Y_{LF} < Y_O < Y_{LH}$: This relationship illustrates the usual relative risks of the legal components of a property. The leasehold position (lessee) in this relationship reflects a combination of all of the possible positions except the lessor and could include one or more sandwich positions along with the occupant (sublessee). While the combined leasehold position (Y_{CLH}) is almost always riskier than Y_O and Y_{LF}, a senior component of the leasehold (first sandwich, for example) could be less risky than Y_O. It would, however, be more risky than Y_{LF}. Generally this relationship assumes that contract rent is less than or equal to market rent and takes into consideration that the lessee has signed a legal document agreeing to pay the rent. Thus, it is possible for this relationship to be invalid under certain conditions.

$Y_{INC} = Y_O = Y_{REV}$: This relationship illustrates the usual relative risks of the economic components of a property. Some investors, however, view the reversion as a riskier component because it occurs the farthest in the future or whenever the income is guaranteed by a lease. If this is the case, then $Y_{INC} < Y_O < Y_{REV}$.

PART TWO

Rates and Ratios

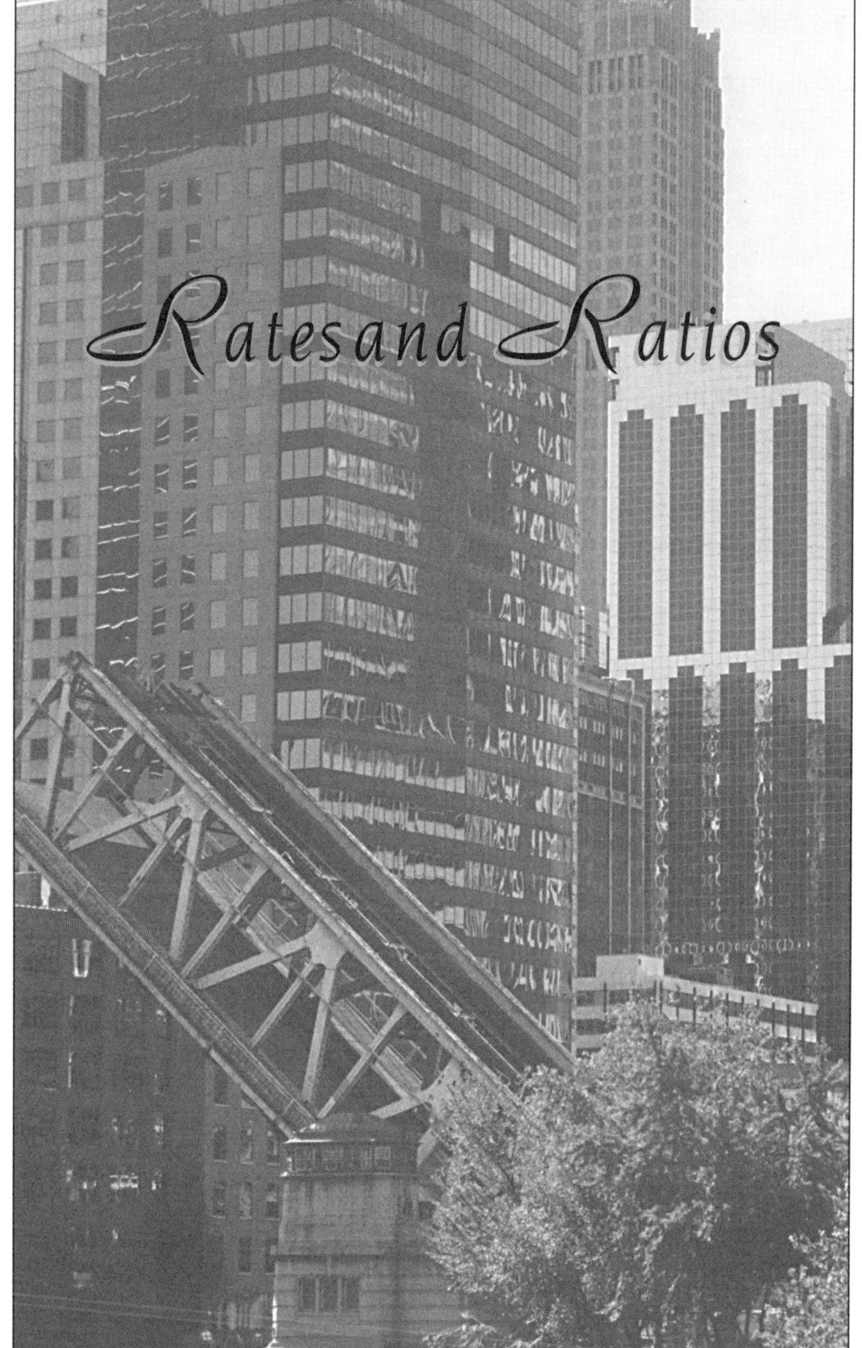

OVERALL CAPITALIZATION RATE

Symbol: R_O

Other names: OAR

Definition: An income rate for a total real property interest that reflects the relationship between a single year's net operating income expectancy and the total property price or value; used to convert net operating income into an indication of overall property value ($R_O = I_O/V_O$).

Description: R_O is the ratio of net operating income (NOI, I_O) to property value (V_O).

Direct use: Converts a single year's net operating income into a property value estimate using $V_O = I_O / R_O$ or converts a property value into an appropriate net operating income using $I_O = R_O \times V_O$.

Other uses: Can be used to estimate a property discount rate (Y_O) using $Y_O = R_O + \Delta \times a$. Can also be used to extract R_E, R_L, and R_B from a sale using the band-of-investment relationship.

Relationship of R_O to

- **R_E:** R_O can be greater than, equal to, or less than R_E depending on R_M. This describes leverage based on cash flows.
- **R_M:** R_O can be greater than, equal to, or less than R_M depending on interest rate and loan term. Also leverage based on cash flows.
- **Y_O:** R_O can be greater than, equal to, or less than Y_O depending on whether V_O is expected to decrease, remain stable, or increase respectively according to $R_O = Y_O - \Delta_O \times a$.

How obtained: Can be extracted from sales using the relationship $R_O = I_O/V_O$ (see Example 1, Part 3). Can also be estimated using the band of investment (financial [see Example 2, Part 3] or physical components) or one of the following formulas:

$R_O = Y_O - \Delta_O \times a$

$R_O = NIR/GIM$

$R_O = M \times R_M \times DCR$

$R_O = [Y_E - M(Y_E + P \times SFF - R_M) - \Delta_O \times 1/S_{\overline{n}|}]/IAF$

where IAF is an income adjustment factor

Cautions: R_O should be extracted from a sale *after* a cash equivalency adjustment. For consistency, if extracted from a sale and applied to the next year's income of a subject property, R_O should reflect the expected next year's NOI of the sale property. If the formula $R_O = NIR/GIM$ is used, the income (I) in NIR and GIM must be consistent, either both potential or both effective. R_O can be extracted and applied with or without the consideration of a replacement allowance as long as both the extraction and application are consistent.

PROPERTY (OVERALL) YIELD RATE

Symbol: Y_O

Other names: Yield rates are sometimes referred to as risk rates, "return on" rates, internal rates of return, interest rates, and discount rates. Y_O, therefore, could be referred to by any of these names if it is used to describe a yield rate for the entire property.

Definition: A rate of return on capital, usually expressed as a compound annual percentage rate. A yield rate considers all expected property benefits, including the proceeds from sale at the termination of the investment. Yield rates include the interest rate, discount rate, internal rate of return (IRR), overall yield rate (Y_O), and equity yield rate (Y_E).

Description: Y_O is the "return on" rate associated with an investment in the entire property. Whenever considered without financing as an analysis tool, $Y_E = Y_O$.

Direct use: Used to value a whole property (not components) by serving either as a discount rate for all future cash flows or as an input variable for the yield capitalization formula $R_O = Y_O - \Delta_O$ x a.

Other uses: Can be used as a limit for other important discount rates (see relationship to other rates below).

Relationship of Y_O to

R_O: Y_O can be greater than, equal to, or less than R_O depending on whether V_O is expected to increase, remain stable, or decrease respectively according to $R_O = Y_O - \Delta_O$ x a.

Y_M: Y_O should be greater than Y_M.

Y_E: Y_O should be less than Y_E.

Y_{LF}: Y_O is usually greater than Y_{LF}.

Y_{LH}: Y_O is usually less than Y_{LH}.

How obtained: Can be extracted from sales of similar properties (see Example 3, Part 3, and Example A, Part 4). Can be estimated using $Y_O = R_O + \Delta_O$ x a, by surveys of market participants, or by comparison with alternative investments (see Example 4, Part 3).

Cautions: Y_O should be extracted from a sale *after* a cash equivalency adjustment. Estimation by comparison with alternative investments is difficult without a study over time of the relationship of Y_O with the yields on the alternate investments. Building a Y_O by adding increments for management, liquidity, risk, etc., to a safe rate is more theoretical than practical. Blending a Y_M and a Y_E to obtain a Y_O by the band-of-investment technique is mathematically incorrect unless the loan is "interest only" and there is no change in income or value (see Example 5, Part 3).

LAND CAPITALIZATION RATE

Symbol: R_L

Other names: None known.

Definition: An income rate for the land portion of real property that reflects the relationship between a single year's net income expectancy attributable to land and the value of land; used to convert income into value or value into income according to the relationship $I_L = R_L \times V_L$.

Description: R_L is associated with one of the physical components (land) of property; therefore, it usually occurs in conjunction with building (improvements) components.

Direct use: Converts a single year's income (I_L) attributable to land into a land value estimate (V_L) using $V_L = I_L/R_L$ or converts a land value (V_L) into an appropriate land cash flow or rent (I_L) using $I_L = R_L \times V_L$.

Other uses: Used in one form of the band-of-investment technique to derive an overall capitalization rate (R_O). Also used in either the land or building residual technique.

Relationship of R_L to

R_O: R_L is usually less than R_O due to recapture.
R_B: R_L is usually less than R_B due to recapture.
Y_L: R_L can be greater than, equal to, or less than Y_L depending on whether V_L is expected to decrease, remain stable, or increase respectively according to $R_L = Y_L - \Delta_L \times a$.

How obtained: Usually extracted from sales using the relationship $R_L = I_L/V_L$ or a variation of the band-of-investment technique (see Example 6, Part 3).

Cautions: R_L should be extracted from a sale *after* a cash equivalency adjustment.

LAND YIELD RATE

Symbol: Y_L

Other names: Yield rates are sometimes referred to as risk rates, "return on" rates, internal rates of return, interest rates, and discount rates. Y_L, therefore, could be referred to by any of these names if it is used to describe a yield rate for the investment in land.

Definition: A rate of return on capital invested in the land portion of real property, usually expressed as a compound annual percentage rate. Considers all expected cash flows attributable to the land investment, including proceeds from sale at the termination of the investment.

Description: Y_L is the "return on" rate associated with an investment in vacant land or where land makes up a portion of the investment (improved property).

Direct use: Used to value land by serving either as a discount rate for all future land cash flows or as an input variable for the yield capitalization formula $R_L = Y_L - \Delta_L \times a$.

Other uses: Used to derive a land capitalization rate (R_L) with the Ellwood formula.

Relationship of Y_L to

- **Y_O:** Y_L is usually the same as Y_O as most investors do not split risk between land and improvements.
- **Y_B:** Y_L is usually the same as Y_B as most investors do not split risk between land and improvements.
- **R_L:** Y_L can be greater than, equal to, or less than R_L depending on whether V_L is expected to increase, remain stable, or decrease respectively according to $R_L = Y_L - \Delta_L \times a$.

How obtained: Since $Y_L = Y_O = Y_B$ is virtually always true, the same techniques used to derive Y_O are true for Y_L (see Property Yield Rate).

Cautions: Y_L should be extracted from a sale *after* a cash equivalency adjustment.

BUILDING CAPITALIZATION RATE

Symbol: R_B

Other names: None known.

Definition: An income rate for the building portion of real property that reflects the relationship between a single year's net income expectancy attributable to the building and the value of the building; used to convert income into value or value into income according the the relationship $I_B = R_B \times V_B$.

Description: R_B is associated with one of the physical components (building) of property. Therefore, it usually occurs in conjunction with a land component.

Direct use: Converts a single year's income (I_B) attributable to the building into a building value estimate (V_B) using $V_B = I_B/R_B$ or converts a building value (V_B) into an appropriate building cash flow or rent (I_B) using $I_B = R_B \times V_B$.

Other uses: Used in one form of the band-of-investment technique to derive an overall capitalization rate (R_O). Also used in either the land or building residual technique.

Relationship of R_B to

R_O: R_B is usually greater than R_O due to recapture.
R_L: R_B is usually greater than R_L due to recapture.
Y_B: R_B can be greater than, equal to, or less than Y_B depending on whether V_B is expected to decrease, remain stable, or increase respectively according to $R_B = Y_B - \Delta_B \times a$.

How obtained: Usually extracted from sales using the relationship $R_B = I_B/V_B$ (see Example 7, Part 3) or a variation of the band of investment.

Cautions: R_B should be extracted from a sale *after* a cash equivalency adjustment.

BUILDING YIELD RATE

Symbol: Y_B

Other names: Yield rates are sometimes referred to as risk rates, "return on" rates, internal rates of return, interest rates, and discount rates. Y_B, therefore, could be referred to by any of these names if it is used to describe a yield rate for the investment in a building.

Definition: A rate of return on capital invested in the building portion of real property, usually expressed as a compound annual percentage rate. Considers all expected cash flows attributable to the building investment, including proceeds from sale at the termination of the investment.

Description: Y_B is the "return on" rate associated with an investment in a building or where a building makes up a portion of the investment (land and building).

Direct use: Used to value a building component by serving either as a discount rate for all future building cash flows or as an input variable for the yield capitalization formula $R_B = Y_B - \Delta_B \times a$.

Other uses: Used to derive a building capitalization rate (R_B) with the Ellwood formula.

Relationship of Y_B to

- **Y_O:** Y_B is usually the same as Y_O as most investors do not split risk between land and improvements.
- **Y_L:** Y_B is usually the same as Y_L as most investors do not split risk between land and improvements.
- **R_B:** Y_B can be greater than, equal to, or less than R_B depending on whether V_B is expected to increase, remain stable, or decrease respectively according to $R_B = Y_B - \Delta_B \times a$.

How obtained: Since $Y_L = Y_O = Y_B$ is virtually always true, the same techniques used to derive Y_O are true for Y_B (see Property Yield Rate).

Cautions: Y_B should be extracted from a sale *after* a cash equivalency adjustment.

MORTGAGE CAPITALIZATION RATE

Symbol: R_M

Other names: Mortgage constant

Definition: The capitalization rate for debt; the ratio of the annual debt service to the principal amount of the mortgage loan. A mortgage constant may be calculated on the basis of the initial mortgage amount or the outstanding mortgage amount; also called mortgage capitalization rate (R_M = debt service/mortgage principal).

Description: R_M is associated with one of the financial components (mortgage) of property. Therefore, it usually occurs in conjunction with an equity component (R_E).

Direct use: Converts a single year's mortgage income (debt service) into a mortgage value using $V_M = I_M / R_M$, or converts a mortgage value (principal amount) into an appropriate mortgage cash flow using $I_M = R_M \times V_M$.

Other uses: Used in one form of the band-of-investment technique to derive an overall capitalization rate (R_O).

Relationship of R_M to

R_O: R_M can be greater than, equal to, or less than R_O depending on interest rate and loan term. This describes leverage based on cash flows.

R_E: R_M can be greater than, equal to, or less than R_E depending on interest rate and loan term. Also leverage based on cash flows.

Y_M: R_M is usually greater than Y_M due to amortization of the loan (recapture). It could be equal to or less than Y_M for an interest-only loan or a negative amortization loan respectively according to $R_M = Y_M - \Delta_M \times a$.

How obtained: Usually obtained by interviewing lenders for loan terms and interest rates. As a fraction, R_M is mathematically equivalent to the annual debt service necessary to amortize a $1 loan (see Example 8, Part 3). Can also be extracted from a sale using the relationship $R_M = I_M/V_M$ (see Example 9, Part 3).

Cautions: R_M should be extracted from a sale *before* a cash equivalency adjustment. R_M is sensitive to interest rates and amortization periods.

MORTGAGE YIELD RATE

Symbol: Y_M

Other names: Interest rate (if no points or other charges increase the lender's yield).

Definition: A rate of return on capital invested as a loan on real property, usually expressed as a compound annual percentage rate. Considers all expected cash flows attributable to the mortgage, including payments, origination fees, prepayment penalties, balloon payments, etc.

Description: Y_M is associated with one of the financial components (mortgage) of property; therefore, it usually occurs in conjunction with an equity component.

Direct use: If equal to the mortgage interest rate, it is used to calculate the mortgage capitalization rate (R_M).

Other uses: Establishes a lower limit for Y_O.

Relationship Y_M to

R_M: Y_M is less than R_M for an amortizing loan. Could be equal to or greater than for an interest-only or a negative amortizing loan.

Y_O: Y_M should be less than Y_O.

Y_E: Y_M should be less than Y_E.

How obtained: Usually obtained by interviewing lenders for interest rate, fees charged (points, prepayment penalties, etc.), and expected loan term (see Example 10, Part 3).

Cautions: Y_M will be higher than the loan interest rate if points or other charges are imposed by the lender. Y_M is sensitive to the number of points and to the anticipated term of the loan.

EQUITY CAPITALIZATION RATE

Symbol: R_E

Other names: Equity dividend rate, cash-on-cash rate, cash-flow rate.

Definition: An income rate for the equity interest in real property that reflects the relationship between a single year's net income expectancy attributable to equity and the value of the equity; used to convert income into value or value into income according to the relationship $I_E = R_E \times V_E$.

Description: R_E is associated with one of the financial components (equity) of property; therefore, it usually occurs in conjunction with mortgage components. Whenever considered without financing as an analysis tool, $R_E = R_O$.

Direct use: Converts a single year's equity income (I_E) into an estimated equity value (V_E) using $V_E = I_E/R_E$ or converts an equity value (V_E) into an appropriate equity cash flow (I_E) using $I_E = R_E \times V_E$.

Other uses: Used in one form of the band-of-investment technique to derive an overall capitalization rate (R_O).

Relationship of R_E to

R_O: R_E can be greater than, equal to, or less than R_O depending on R_M.

R_M: R_E can be greater than, equal to, or less than R_M depending on the interest rate and loan term.

Y_E: R_E can be greater than, equal to, or less than Y_E depending on whether V_E is expected to decrease, remain stable, or increase respectively according to $R_E = Y_E - \Delta_E \times a$.

How obtained: Usually extracted from sales using the relationship $R_E = I_E/V_E$ or a variation of the band of investment (see Example 11, Part 3). Can also be estimated by surveys of market participants.

Cautions: R_E should be extracted from a sale *before* a cash equivalency adjustment. R_E is extremely sensitive to loan-to-value ratios and amortization periods.

EQUITY YIELD RATE

Symbol: Y_E

Other names: Yield rates are sometimes referred to as risk rates, "return on" rates, internal rates of return, interest rates, and discount rates. Y_E, therefore, could be referred to by any of these names if it is used to describe a yield rate for an equity investment.

Definition: A rate of return on capital invested in the equity position of real property, usually expressed as a compound annual percentage rate. Considers all expected cash flows attributable to the equity investment, including proceeds from sale at the termination of the investment.

Description: Y_E is the "return on" rate associated with equity investment in a property. Whenever considered without financing as an analysis tool, $Y_E = Y_O$.

Direct use: Used to value the equity position by serving either as a discount rate for all future equity cash flows or as an input variable for the yield capitalization formula $R_E = Y_E - \Delta_E \times a$.

Other uses: Used to derive an overall capitalization rate (R_O) with the Ellwood formula. Also used to establish an upper limit for Y_O.

Relationship of Y_E to

Y_O: Y_E should be greater than Y_O.
Y_M: Y_E should be greater than Y_M.
R_E: Y_E can be greater than, equal to, or less than R_E depending on whether V_E is expected to increase, remain stable, or decrease respectively according to $R_E = Y_E - \Delta_E \times a$.

How obtained: Can be extracted from sales of similar properties (see Example 12, Part 3, and Example B, Part 4) or estimated by surveys of market participants.

Cautions: Y_E should be extracted from a sale *before* a cash equivalency adjustment. Y_E is extremely sensitive to loan-to-value ratios. Blending a Y_M and a Y_E to obtain a Y_O by the band of investment is mathematically incorrect unless the loan is "interest only" and there is no change in income and value.

LEASED FEE CAPITALIZATION RATE

Symbol: R_{LF}

Other names: None known.

Definition: An income rate for a leased fee interest in real property that reflects the relationship between a single year's net income expectancy attributable to the leased fee interest and the value of the leased fee interest; used to convert income into value or value into income according the the relationship $I_{LF} = R_{LF} \times V_{LF}$.

Description: R_{LF} expresses the ratio of the leased fee income (I_{LF}) and the value of the leased fee (V_{LF}).

Direct use: Converts a single year's leased fee income (I_{LF}) into an estimated leased fee value (V_{LF}) using $V_{LF} = I_{LF} / R_{LF}$, or converts a leased fee value (V_{LF}) into an appropriate leased fee cash flow or rent (I_{LF}) using $I_{LF} = R_{LF} \times V_{LF}$.

Other uses: None known.

Relationship of R_{LF} to

R_O: R_{LF} is usually less than R_O.

R_{SAND}: R_{LF} is usually less than R_{SAND}.

R_{LH}: R_{LF} is usually less than R_{LH}.

Y_{LF}: R_{LF} can be greater than, equal to, or less than Y_{LF} depending on whether V_{LF} is expected to decrease, remain stable, or increase respectively according to $R_{LF} = Y_{LF} - \Delta_{LF} \times a$.

How obtained: Usually extracted from sales using the relationship $R_{LF} = I_{LF} / V_{LF}$.

Cautions: R_{LF} should be extracted from a sale after a *cash* equivalency adjustment. R_{LF} is unreliable unless the lease terms of the sale property are extremely similar to the lease terms of the subject property. As a result, leased fee positions are typically valued with a yield capitalization technique using a Y_{LF}.

LEASED FEE YIELD RATE

Symbol: Y_{LF}

Other names: Yield rates are sometimes referred to as risk rates, "return on" rates, internal rates of return, interest rates, and discount rates. Y_{LF}, therefore, could be referred to by any of these names if it is used to describe a yield rate for the investment in a leased fee interest.

Definition: A rate of return on capital invested in a leased fee position in real property, usually expressed as a compound annual percentage rate. Considers all expected cash flows attributable to the leased fee position, including proceeds from sale at the termination of the investment.

Description: Y_{LF} is the "return on" rate associated with an investment in the leased fee position.

Direct use: Used to value a leased fee position in a property by serving as a discount rate for all future cash flows associated with the leased fee position.

Other uses: Can be used as a limit for other important discount rates (see relationship to other rates below).

Relationship of Y_{LF} to

- **Y_O:** Y_{LF} is usually less than Y_O due to risk.
- **Y_{SAND}:** Y_{LF} is usually less than Y_{SAND} due to risk.
- **Y_{LH}:** Y_{LF} is usually less than Y_{LH} due to risk.
- **R_{LF}:** Y_{LF} can be greater than, equal to, or less than R_{LF} depending on whether V_{LF} is expected to increase, remain stable, or decrease respectively according to $R_{LF} = Y_{LF} - \Delta_{LF} \times a$.

How obtained: Can be extracted from sales of similar properties (see Example 13, Part 3), estimated by surveys of market participants, or estimated based on Y_O (see Example 14, Part 3).

Cautions: Y_{LF} should be extracted from a sale *after* a cash equivalency adjustment. Risk must be taken into consideration. A leased fee income that is 50% of market rent would likely be discounted at a lower rate than a leased fee income that is 95% of market rent. The credit rating of the tenant(s) should also be taken into consideration.

LEASEHOLD CAPITALIZATION RATE

Symbol: R_{LH}

Other names: None known.

Definition: An income rate for a leasehold interest in real property that reflects the relationship between a single year's net income expectancy attributable to the leasehold interest and the value of the leasehold interest; used to convert income into value or value into income according to the relationship $I_{LH} = R_{LH} \times V_{LH}$.

Description: R_{LH} expresses the ratio of the leasehold income (I_{LH}) and the value of the leasehold position (V_{LH}).

Direct use: Converts a single year's leasehold income (I_{LH}) into an estimate of leasehold value (V_{LH}) using $V_{LH} = I_{LH} / R_{LH}$ or converts a leasehold value (V_{LH}) into an appropriate leasehold cash flow or rent (I_{LH}) using $I_{LH} = R_{LH} \times V_{LH}$.

Other uses: None known.

Relationship of R_{LH} to

R_O: R_{LH} is usually greater than R_O.

R_{LF}: R_{LH} is usually greater than R_{LF}.

R_{SAND}: The sandwich position is a part of a *combined* leasehold position. Due to risk, R_{SAND} is usually less than the capitalization rate for any leasehold positions (other sandwich positions and the sublease position) junior to it.

Y_{LH}: R_{LH} is usually greater than Y_{LH} as leasehold positions usually decline to zero (no reversion).

How obtained: Usually extracted from sales using the relationship $R_{LH} = I_{LH} / V_{LH}$.

Cautions: R_{LH} should be extracted from a sale *after* a cash equivalency adjustment. R_{LH} is unreliable unless the lease terms of the sale property are extremely similar to the lease terms of the subject property. As a result, leasehold positions are typically valued with a yield capitalization technique using a Y_{LH}.

LEASEHOLD YIELD RATE

Symbol: Y_{LH}

Other names: Yield rates are sometimes referred to as risk rates, "return on" rates, internal rates of return, interest rates, and discount rates. Y_{LH}, therefore, could be referred to by any of these names if it is used to describe a yield rate for an investment in a leasehold interest.

Definition: A rate of return on capital invested in a leasehold position in real property, usually expressed as a compound annual percentage rate. Considers all expected cash flows attributable to the leasehold position, including proceeds from sale at the termination of the investment.

Description: Y_{LH} is the "return on" rate associated with an investment in the leasehold position. "Leasehold" refers any of the legal components (other than the leased fee) created by a lease or leases.

Direct use: Used to value a leasehold position in a property by serving as a discount rate for all future cash flows associated with the leasehold position.

Other uses: Can be used as a limit for other important discount rates (see relationship to other rates below).

Relationship of Y_{LH} to

- **Y_O:** Y_{LH} is usually greater than Y_O due to risk.
- **Y_{LF}:** Y_{LH} is usually greater than Y_{LF} due to risk.
- **Y_{SAND}:** The sandwich position is a part of a *combined* leasehold position. Due to risk, Y_{SAND} is usually less than the yield rate for any leasehold positions (other sandwich positions and the subleasehold position) junior to it.
- **R_{LH}:** Y_{LH} is usually less than R_{LH} as leasehold positions typically decline to zero (no reversion).

How obtained: Can be extracted from sales of similar properties, estimated by surveys of market participants, or estimated based on Y_O (see Example 14, Part 3).

Cautions: Y_{LH} should be extracted from a sale *after* a cash equivalency adjustment. Sales of leaseholds are sometimes difficult to find as they are not typically recorded. In addition, sales of leaseholds frequently involve more than real estate (personal property, inventory, business, etc.). Risk must be taken into consideration. Variations in market rent affect the leasehold position before they affect the leased fee income.

SANDWICH CAPITALIZATION RATE

Symbol: R_{SAND}

Other names: None known.

Definition: An income rate for a sandwich position in real property created by leases that reflects the relationship between a single year's net income expectancy attributable to the sandwich position and the value of the sandwich position; used to convert income into value or value into income according to the relationship $I_{SAND} = R_{SAND} \times V_{SAND}$.

Description: R_{SAND} expresses the ratio of the sandwich position's income (I_{SAND}) and the value of the sandwich position (V_{SAND}).

Direct use: Converts a single year's sandwich position income (I_{SAND}) into an estimated sandwich position value (V_{SAND}) using $V_{SAND} = I_{SAND}/R_{SAND}$, or converts a sandwich position value (V_{SAND}) into an appropriate sandwich position cash flow or rent (I_{SAND}) using $I_{SAND} = R_{SAND} \times V_{SAND}$.

Other uses: None known.

Relationship of R_{SAND} to

R_O: Its relationship to R_O is a function of risk and could vary.

R_{LF}: R_{SAND} is usually greater than R_{LF}.

R_{LH}: The sandwich position is a part of a *combined* leasehold position. Due to risk, R_{SAND} is usually less than the capitalization rate for any leasehold positions (other sandwich positions and the sublease position) junior to it.

Y_{SAND}: R_{SAND} can be greater than, equal to, or less than Y_{SAND} depending on whether V_{SAND} is expected to decrease, remain stable, or increase respectively according to $R_{SAND} = Y_{SAND} - \Delta_{SAND} \times a$.

How obtained: Usually extracted from sales using the relationship $R_{SAND} = I_{SAND}/V_{SAND}$.

Cautions: R_{SAND} should be extracted from a sale *after* a cash equivalency adjustment. R_{SAND} is unreliable unless the lease terms of the sale property are extremely similar to the lease terms of the subject property. As a result, sandwich positions are typically valued with a yield capitalization technique using a Y_{SAND}.

SANDWICH YIELD RATE

Symbol: Y_{SAND}

Other names: Yield rates are sometimes referred to as risk rates, "return on" rates, internal rates of return, interest rates, and discount rates. Y_{SAND}, therefore, could be referred to by any of these names if it is used to describe a characteristic of a sandwich interest in the property.

Definition: A rate of return on capital invested in a sandwich position in real property, usually expressed as a compound annual percentage rate. Considers all expected cash flows attributable to the sandwich position, including proceeds from sale at the termination of the investment.

Description: Y_{SAND} is the "return on" rate associated with an investment in a sandwich position. A sandwich position is one of several possible leasehold positions (other than the leased fee) that can be created by a lease or leases.

Direct use: Used to value a sandwich position in a property by serving as a discount rate for all future cash flows associated with the sandwich position.

Other uses: Can be used as a limit for other important discount rates (see relationship to other rates below).

Relationship of Y_{SAND} to

Y_O: Y_{SAND} can be greater than, equal to, or less than Y_O according to risk.

Y_{LF}: Y_{SAND} is usually greater than Y_{LF} due to risk.

Y_{LH}: The sandwich position is a part of a *combined* leasehold position. Due to risk, Y_{SAND} is usually less than the yield rate for any leasehold positions (other sandwich positions and the subleasehold position) junior to it.

R_{LH}: Y_{SAND} is usually less than R_{LH} as sandwich positions typically decline to zero (no reversion).

How obtained: Can be extracted from sales of similar properties, estimated by surveys of market participants, or estimated based on Y_{LF} and the yield rate for the combined leaseholds (see Example 15, Part 3).

Cautions: Y_{SAND} should be extracted from a sale *after* a cash equivalency adjustment. Sales of sandwich positions are sometimes difficult to find as they may not be recorded. In addition, sales of sandwich positions sometimes involve more than real estate (personal property, inventory, business, etc.). Risk must be taken into consideration. Variations in market rent affect any subleasehold position before they affect the sandwich position's income.

SUBLEASEHOLD CAPITALIZATION RATE

Symbol: R_{SLH}

Other names: None known.

Definition: An income rate for a subleasehold position in real property created by leases that reflects the relationship between a single year's net income expectancy attributable to the subleasehold position and the value of the subleasehold position; used to convert income into value or value into income according to the relationship $I_{SLH} = R_{SLH} \times V_{SLH}$.

Description: R_{SLH} is associated with one of the legal components (a potential part of the leasehold interest) of a property. Subleasehold, by definition, refers to the interest created when someone leases from a lessee. There can be, therefore, more than one sublessee if there is more than one sandwich position. In this handbook, however, it refers to the last leasehold position (occupant). R_{SLH} expresses the ratio of the subleasehold's income (I_{SLH}) and the value of the subleasehold position (V_{SLH}).

Direct use: Converts a single year's subleasehold income (I_{SLH}) into an estimated subleasehold value (V_{SLH}) using $V_{SLH} = I_{SLH}/R_{SLH}$, or converts a subleasehold value (V_{SLH}) into an appropriate subleasehold cash flow or rent (I_{SLH}) using $I_{SLH} = R_{SLH} \times V_{SLH}$.

Other uses: None known.

Relationship of R_{SLH} to

R_O: R_{SLH} is usually greater than R_O.

R_{LF}: R_{SLH} is usually greater than R_{LF}.

R_{SAND}: The sandwich position is a part of a *combined* leasehold position. Due to risk, R_{SAND} is usually less than the capitalization rate for any leasehold positions (other sandwich positions and the sublease position) junior to it.

Y_{LH}: R_{SLH} is usually greater than Y_{LH} as leasehold positions usually decline to zero (no reversion).

How obtained: Usually extracted from sales using the relationship $R_{SLH} = I_{SLH}/V_{SLH}$.

Cautions: R_{SLH} should be extracted from a sale *after* a cash equivalency adjustment. R_{SLH} is unreliable unless the sublease terms of the sale property are extremely similar to the sublease terms of the subject property. As a result, leasehold positions are typically valued with a yield capitalization technique using a Y_{SLH}.

SUBLEASEHOLD YIELD RATE

Symbol: Y_{SLH}

Other names: Yield rates are sometimes referred to as risk rates, "return on" rates, internal rates of return, interest rates, and discount rates. Y_{SLH}, therefore, could be referred to by any of these names if it is used to describe a characteristic of the subleasehold interest in the property.

Definition: A rate of return on capital invested in a subleasehold position in real property, usually expressed as a compound annual percentage rate. Considers all expected cash flows attributable to the subleasehold position, including proceeds from sale at the termination of the investment.

Description: Y_{SLH} is associated with one of the legal components (a potential part of the leasehold interest) of a property. Subleasehold, by definition, refers to the interest created when someone leases from a lessee. There can be, therefore, more than one sublessee if there is more than one sandwich position. In this handbook, however, it refers to the last leasehold position (occupant). Y_{SLH} refers to the "return on" rate associated with the subleasehold position.

Direct use: Used to value a subleasehold position in a property by serving as a discount rate for all future benefits (usually in the form of not having to pay full market rent) associated with the subleasehold position.

Other uses: Can be used as a limit for other important discount rates (see relationship to other rates below).

Relationship of Y_{SLH} to

- **Y_O:** Y_{SLH} is usually greater than Y_O due to risk.
- **Y_{SAND}:** Y_{SLH} is usually greater than Y_{SAND} due to risk.
- **Y_{LH}:** Y_{SLH} is usually greater than Y_{LH} due to risk.
- **R_{SLH}:** Y_{SLH} is usually less than R_{SLH} as subleasehold positions typically decline to zero (no reversion).

How obtained: Can be extracted from sales of similar properties, estimated by surveys of market participants, or estimated based on Y_{LF} and the yield rate for the combined leaseholds (see Example 15, Part 3).

Cautions: Y_{SLH} should be extracted from a sale *after* a cash equivalency adjustment. Sales of subleaseholds are sometimes difficult to find as they are not typically recorded. In addition, sales of subleaseholds frequently involve more than real estate (personal property, inventory, business, etc.). Risk must be taken into consideration. Variations in market rent usually affect the subleasehold position before they affect any of the other components created by leases.

INCOME YIELD RATE

Symbol: Y_{INC}

Other names: Yield rates are sometimes referred to as risk rates, "return on" rates, internal rates of return, interest rates, and discount rates. Y_{INC}, therefore, could be referred to by any of these names if it is used to describe a separate analysis of the cash flows from operations (NOIs).

Definition: A rate of return on capital as it applies to that portion of an investment in real property attributable to cash flows from operations (NOIs), usually expressed as a compound annual percentage rate. It explicitly excludes any cash flow attributable to the reversion(s).

Description: Y_{INC} is the "return on" or risk rate associated with that portion of an investment reflected by cash flows from operations (as opposed to cash flow from the reversion).

Direct use: Used to separately value cash flows from operations by serving as a discount rate for all future cash flows from operations.

Other uses: None known.

Relationship of Y_{INC} to

Y_O: Y_{INC} can be greater than, equal to, or less than Y_O depending on the perceived risk relationship of the economic components. However, it might be considered less than Y_O due to one of the following reasons:

1) The cash flows from operations are "guaranteed" by a lessee with a good credit rating whereas the reversion is a function of future market forces.
2) Investors associate less risk with forecasting benefits earlier in time compared to forecasting a reversion, which is usually the farthest in the future.

Y_{REV}: Y_{INC} is usually less than Y_{REV} for the reasons noted above.

R_{INC}: R_{INC} is not typically used as a valuation tool.

How obtained: Can be extracted from a sale if sufficient information is available (see Example 16, Part 3). The two-variable extraction technique may offer the best tool for extraction (see Examples A and B, Part 4). Can be estimated by surveys of market participants.

Cautions: Y_{INC} should be extracted from a sale *after* a cash equivalency adjustment. Separately valuing the economic components of a property (except for a leased fee interest) is a relatively new concept. If used, the technique should not produce a value different than if a single discount rate (Y_O) were used. Thus if Y_{INC} is not equal to Y_{REV}, neither is it equal to Y_O.

REVERSION YIELD RATE

Symbol: Y_{REV}

Other names: Yield rates are sometimes referred to as risk rates, "return on" rates, internal rates of return, interest rates, and discount rates. Y_{REV}, therefore, could be referred to by any of these names if it is used to describe a separate analysis of the reversion.

Definition: A rate of return on capital as it applies to that portion of an investment in real property attributable to the cash flow(s) from the reversion, usually expressed as a compound annual percentage rate. It explicitly excludes any cash flow attributable to the operations (NOIs).

Description: Y_{REV} is the "return on" or risk rate associated with that portion of an investment reflected by the reversion (as opposed to cash flows from operating income).

Direct use: Used to separately value the cash flow from a reversion by serving as a discount rate for the expected reversion.

Other uses: None known.

Relationship of Y_{REV} to

Y_O: Y_{REV} can be greater than, equal to, or less than Y_O depending on the perceived risk relationship of the economic components. However, it might be considered greater than Y_O due to one of the following reasons:

1) The cash flows from operations are "guaranteed" by a lessee with a good credit rating, whereas the reversion is a function of future market forces.
2) Investors associate less risk with forecasting benefits earlier in time compared to forecasting a reversion, which is usually the farthest in the future.

Y_{INC}: Y_{REV} is usually greater than Y_{INC} for the reasons noted above.

R_{REV}: R_{REV} is not typically used as a valuation tool.

How obtained: Can be extracted from a sale if sufficient information is available (see Example 16, Part 3). The two-variable extraction technique may offer the best tool for extraction (see Examples A and B, Part 4). Can be estimated by surveys of market participants.

Cautions: Y_{REV} should be extracted from a sale *after* a cash equivalency adjustment. Separately valuing the economic components of a property (except for a leased fee interest) is a relatively new concept. If used, the technique should not produce a value different than if a single discount rate (Y_O) were used. Thus, if Y_{REV} is not equal to Y_{INC}, neither is it equal to Y_O.

TERMINAL CAPITALIZATION RATE

Symbol: R_N

Other names: Residual capitalization rate

Definition: The rate used to convert income, i.e., NOI or cash flow, into an indication of the anticipated value of the subject property at the end of the holding period; used to estimate the resale value of the property.

Description: R_N is used by investors to estimate the reversionary value of a property. It is usually greater than the "going in" capitalization rate (R_O) due to one or both of the following reasons:

1) The investor, recognizing the importance of the reversion in the success of an investment and attempting to reduce the risk of uncertainty, forecasts a selling price using a terminal capitalization rate that is higher than the purchase capitalization rate;
2) If an investment property is improved, the improvements will be closer to the end of their economic life at the end of the holding period. Thus the subsequent buyers will have shorter and shorter recapture periods for that portion of the investment attributable to the improvements. Since capitalization rates are a function of both yield and recapture, they tend to increase over time for improved properties.

Direct use: Used in discounted cash flow analysis to estimate the amount of the reversion.

Other uses: None known.

Relationship of R_N to R_O: R_N can be greater than or equal to R_O but is rarely less than R_O (the "going in" capitalization rate).

How obtained: Interviews with market participants.

Cautions: Terminal capitalization rates affect yields. Care should be taken regarding the selection of the incremental difference between "going in" and terminal capitalization rates.

LOAN-TO-VALUE RATIO

Symbol: M

Other names: None known.

Definition: The ratio between a mortgage loan and the value of the property pledged as security; usually expressed as a percentage.

Description: A lender's tool to reduce risk. A 70% loan-to-value ratio offers protection to the lender by allowing a property value to decrease by 30% (more if amortization has taken place) and still have the property (collateral) cover the loan amount.

Direct use: Serves as a basis for an upper limit of a loan amount.

Other uses: Used by appraisers for analysis purposes. Necessary in the following techniques or formulas:

band of investment

$R_O = M \times R_M \times DCR$

$R_O = Y_E - M[Y_E + P \times 1/S_{\overline{n}|} - R_M) - \Delta_O \times 1/S_{\overline{n}|}]/IAF$

Relationship of M to other rates: Usually less than 100%

How obtained: Interviews with active lenders. Can be extracted from sales by dividing the loan amount by the selling price.

Cautions: The loan-to-value ratio is a major component in the analysis of leverage, based on either cash flows or yields. The impact (not type) of leverage is very sensitive to the magnitude of the loan-to-value ratio. Generally, loan-to-value ratios obtained from lender interviews are more meaningful if a new loan is assumed in the appraisal analysis. In unusual mortgage markets, however, institutional lenders' terms may not be acceptable to the prudent investor.

DEBT COVERAGE RATIO

Symbol: DCR

Other names: Debt service coverage ratio

Definition: The ratio of net operating income to annual debt service; measures the ability of a property to meet its debt service out of net operating income.

Description: A lender's tool to reduce risk. A debt coverage ratio of 1.25 offers protection to the lender because the NOI generated by the property is 25% higher than the debt service.

Direct use: Serves as a basis for an upper limit of a loan amount.

Other uses: Used by appraisers for analysis purposes. Necessary in the formula $R_O = M \times R_M \times DCR$.

Relationship of DCR to other rates: Usually greater than 1.0.

How obtained: Interviews with active lenders. Can be extracted from sales by dividing the net operating income by the debt service.

Cautions: To avoid factual inconsistencies, the appraiser could calculate the DCR implied by the data in the appraisal report. Thus, the debt coverage ratio is an ideal "test of reasonableness."

LAND-TO-PROPERTY VALUE RATIO

Symbol: L

Other names: None known.

Definition: The ratio between land value and total property value, usually expressed as a percentage.

Description: L is associated with one of the physical components (land) of property.

Direct use: Used in the band-of-investment technique either to estimate an overall capitalization rate (R_O) or to extract a land capitalization rate (R_L) or a building capitalization rate (R_B).

Other uses: None known.

Relationship of L to other rates: Less than 100% for improved property if improvements have value.

How obtained: Extraction from sales or interviews with knowledgeable investors.

Cautions: This term should not be confused with a land-to-building ratio, which is a ratio of land size to building size.

BUILDING-TO-PROPERTY VALUE RATIO

Symbol: B

Other names: None known.

Definition: The ratio between building value and total property value, usually expressed as a percentage.

Description: B is associated with one of the physical components (building) of property.

Direct Use: Used in the band-of-investment technique either to estimate an overall capitalization rate (R_O) or to extract a land capitalization rate (R_L) or a building capitalization rate (R_B).

Other uses: None known.

Relationship of B to other rates: Less than 100%

How obtained: Extraction from sales or interviews with knowledgeable investors.

Cautions: This term should not be confused with a land-to-building ratio, which is a ratio of land size to building size.

OPERATING EXPENSE RATIO

Symbol: OER

Other names: Expense ratio

Definition: The ratio of total operating expenses to effective gross income (TOE/EGI); the complement of the net income ratio, i.e., 1 - NIR.

Description: See definition.

Direct use: Used in the estimate of net operating income (NOI).

Other uses: Used as a "test of reasonableness" of the operating expense estimated in a reconstructed operating statement.

Relationship of OER to other rates: The complement of the net income ratio (NIR).

How obtained: Analysis of operating statements of similar properties, i.e., the subject property and comparable properties.

Cautions: The definition and most applications base this ratio on effective gross income. The market, however, may calculate it based on potential gross income. The difference may be significant if vacancy and collection loss is a relatively large percentage.

NET INCOME RATIO

Symbol:	NIR
Other names:	Expense ratio
Definition:	The ratio of net operating income to effective gross income (NOI/EGI); the complement of the operating expense ratio, i.e., 1 - OER.
Description:	See definition.
Direct use:	Used in the estimate of net operating income (NOI).
Other uses:	Used as a "test of reasonableness" of the operating expense estimated in a reconstructed operating statement.
Relationship of NIR to other rates:	The complement of the operating expense ratio (OER).
How obtained:	Analysis of operating statements of similar properties, i.e., the subject property and comparable properties.
Cautions:	The definition and most applications base this ratio on effective gross income. The market, however, may calculate it based on potential gross income. The difference may be significant if vacancy and collection loss is a relatively large percentage.

PART THREE

Rate Extraction Examples

Example 1: Extracting an R_O from a Sale

A property sold for $375,000 with an expected potential gross income of $73,000 during the first year of ownership. Vacancy and collection loss has been estimated at 4.5% and expenses are expected to be 39% of effective gross income. What overall capitalization rate (R_O) can be extracted?

Solution

Potential gross income	$73,000
Vacancy & collection loss (4.5%)	3,285
Effective gross income	$69,715
Expenses (39%)	27,189
Net operating income	$42,526

$$R_O = I_O / V_O$$
$$R_O = \$42{,}526 / \$375{,}000$$
$$= 0.1134, \text{ or } 11.34\%$$

Comment

If $375,000 had not been the cash equivalent purchase price, the resultant R_O would have been different and incorrect. Also, because R_Os are virtually always applied to the first year NOI of a subject property, the $42,526 above must be the sale's first year NOI to be consistent.

Example 2: Estimating R_O Using Mortgage-Equity Band-of-Investment Technique

Several sales were analyzed to extract an equity capitalization rate (R_E) as follows:

Sale	Loan-to-value ratio	R_E	Term
1	60%	7.3%	18 yrs.
2	90%	1.9%	22 yrs.
3	75%	5.4%	20 yrs.

The subject property is eligible for a 70% loan at 9.25% interest amortized over 20 years with monthly payments. What R_O would be derived by the band-of-investment technique?

Solution

The market, as evidenced by the sales, suggests that equity capitalization rates are sensitive to loan-to-value ratios indicating negative

---

Note: Solutions to the problems in these examples have been determined by keystrokes from an HP or similar calculator.

leverage based on cash flows. A 6.0% R_E for a 70% loan appears consistent with the market. Therefore:

Mortgage	0.70 x 0.1099	=	0.0769
Equity	0.30 x 0.0600	=	0.0180
	R_O	=	0.0949

Comment

The layout above is mathematically equivalent to the formula $R_O = M \times R_M + (1 - M) \times R_E$.

EXAMPLE 3: EXTRACTING A Y_O FROM A SALE

A property sold for $300,000 with an expected net operating income of $36,000 during the first year of ownership. The buyer indicated an expected increase in income and value of 3% per year over the next five years. What property yield rate (Y_O) can be extracted?

Solution

Income is changing at a constant ratio, therefore, $R_O = Y_O - CR$ is the proper relationship. R_O = 12% and CR = 3%. Thus:

$$R_O = Y_O - CR$$
$$0.12 = Y_O - 0.03$$
$$Y_O = 0.15 \text{ or } 15\%$$

Comment

Implicit in the use of this formula is the fact that both income and value are changing at the same compound rate. This also means that the terminal capitalization rate (R_N) and R_O are the same.

EXAMPLE 4: ESTIMATING A Y_O USING ALTERNATIVE INVESTMENTS

Theoretically relationships exist between yields on various alternative investments (bonds, mortgages, treasury bills, etc.) and real estate. If these relationships are charted over time to determine if a pattern exists, and if yield rates of one or more of the alternative investments are known as of the appraisal date, an estimate of the real estate yield rate may be possible. For example:

Year	Quarter	Y_O	Indicator 1	Indicator 2	Indicator 3
1990	1	11.11%	10.10%	9.37%	8.63%
1990	2	11.71%	10.21%	9.20%	8.67%
1990	3	11.87%	10.74%	9.63%	8.21%
1990	4	12.24%	10.21%	9.02%	8.22%
1991	1	11.78%	10.37%	8.93%	8.36%
1991	2	12.12%	10.54%	9.05%	8.55%
1991	3	12.21%	9.92%	8.58%	7.88%
1991	4	12.34%	9.51%	8.34%	7.64%
1992	1	12.06%	9.67%	8.36%	7.91%
1992	2	12.21%	9.41%	8.17%	7.68%
1992	3	12.49%	8.71%	7.94%	7.13%
1992	4	12.42%	8.98%	7.91%	7.29%
1993	1	12.18%	8.40%	7.62%	6.60%
1993	2	12.10%	8.25%	7.23%	6.47%
1993	3	12.05%	7.80%	6.68%	5.87%
1993	4	11.86%	7.85%	6.91%	6.18%

An analysis of the chart reveals that, over the entire period, the mean difference between Y_Os and indicators 1, 2, and 3 have been 2.63%, 3.74%, and 4.47% respectively. Over the last four quarters, the differences have been 3.97%, 4.94%, and 5.77%. If the yields on the three indicators are known as of the appraisal date, the appraiser may be able to offer support for the selection of a Y_O.

Comment

The disadvantage of this technique is that not all real estate investments have the same inherent risk and that the proper discount rate is also a function of the type of forecast made, e.g., conservative, middle of the road, or liberal. This technique, therefore, is not usually used as a primary source for estimating yield rates.

Example 5: Demonstrating Error Inherent in the Use of the Band-of-Investment Technique to Estimate a Y_O.

A property is to be appraised using discounted cash flow analysis. The NOIs for the next five years have been forecast as $15,000, $15,500, $16,500, $17,000, and $18,000. In addition, a reversion of $175,000 is expected. A 70% loan with an interest rate of 9% for 20 years is available with annual payments. The appropriate equity yield rate (Y_E) is 16%.

Application of a band-of-investment technique to calculate a property yield rate (Y_O) would be as follows:

Mortgage	0.70 x 9%	=	0.0630
Equity	0.30 x 16%	=	0.0480
Apparent Y_O		=	0.1110, or 11.10%

Comment

Using this apparent Y_O the value of the property would be $163,271. The equity yield rate (Y_E), however, will not be 16% as expected. See below.

Year	Property cash flows	Mortgage cash flows	Equity cash flows
0	-163,271	-114,289	-48,981
1	15,000	12,520	2,480
2	15,500	12,520	2,980
3	16,500	12,520	3,480
4	17,000	12,520	4,480
5	18,000	12,520	5,480
Rev	175,000	100,920	74,080

The internal rate of return for the equity position (Y_E) above can be calculated to be 14.91%, or 1.09% less than the 16% expected by the market. The primary reason the equity yield rates were not the same is the fact that the loan-to-value ratio (M) is not the same throughout the holding period. The band-of-investment technique, therefore, is not reliable for estimating yield rates.

EXAMPLE 6: EXTRACTING AN R_L FROM SALES DATA

Ideally, to estimate a land capitalization rate the appraiser has access to information on the sale of a site that has just been rented. In practice, however, the appraiser may have to combine data to estimate an R_L.

Suppose a commercial site has just been leased for \$1.20 per square foot per year and a nearby site (virtually identical) has just sold for \$14.00 per square foot. The following R_L can be extracted:

$$\begin{aligned} R_L &= I_L/V_L \\ &= \$1.20/\$14.00 \\ &= 0.0857 \end{aligned}$$

Comment

Care must be taken in an analysis such as this to be sure that the assumptions made are reasonable, i.e., it is appropriate to match two transactions to extract one rate. Also, the selling price used should be the cash equivalent selling price.

EXAMPLE 7: EXTRACTING AN R_B FROM SALES DATA

An improved property sold for \$150,000 with an expected first year NOI of \$15,750 and an estimated land value of \$30,000. If R_L is 9%, what is R_B?

Solution

$$\begin{aligned} I_L &= R_L \text{ x } V_L \\ &= 0.09 \text{ x } 30{,}000 = 2{,}700 \\ \text{therefore} \quad I_B &= NOI - I_L \\ &= 15{,}750 - 2{,}700 = 13{,}050 \\ \text{Also} \quad V_B &= V_O - V_L \\ &= 150{,}000 - 30{,}000 = 120{,}000 \\ \text{Thus} \quad R_B &= I_B/V_B \\ &= 13{,}050/120{,}000 = 0.1088 \\ &= 10.88\% \end{aligned}$$

Comment

The selling price used should be the cash equivalent selling price.

Example 8: Calculating R_M Based on Mortgage Terms

Typical mortgage terms in an area are as follows:

Loan-to-value ratio	70%
Interest rate	9%
Term	20 years
Payments	monthly

R_M, as a fraction, is mathematically equivalent to the *annual* debt service necessary to amortize a $1.00 loan. Thus, n = 240 months, i = 0.75%, PV = -1, and FV = 0. Solving for PMT results in a monthly payment of 0.008997. The annual debt service is 12 times this number or 0.107964.

Comment

The mortgage terms used in this analysis are typically obtained by interviewing lenders active in the market where the subject property is located.

Example 9: Extracting R_M from a Sale

A property sold for $650,000 with an assumed loan of $425,113 at 9.65% interest. Monthly debt service was $4,310.22. What R_M can be extracted from this transaction?

Solution

$$R_M = I_M/V_M$$
$$= (\$4{,}310.22 \times 12)/\$425{,}113$$
$$= 0.121668$$

Comment:

The $650,000 used above should *not* have been adjusted for cash equivalency because the amount invested (equity and lender) is actually $650,000 ($224,887 + $425,113). R_E and R_M must be based on actual prices paid.

EXAMPLE 10: CALCULATING A Y_M

A \$100,000 loan for 20 years with monthly payments is made with an interest rate of 9% and a loan origination fee of three points. What will the lender's yield be if the loan runs full term? If the loan is paid off in three years?

Solution

The monthly payment is \$899.73.

The lender's investment is actually \$97,000 (\$100,000 - \$3,000).

The balance in three years will be \$93,838.

If the loan runs full term, Y_M is 9.43% (n = 240, PV = -97,000, PMT = 899.73, FV = 0, solve for i, multiply by 12).

If the loan is paid off in three years, Y_M is 10.20% (n = 36, PV = -97,000, PMT = 899.73, FV = 93,838, solve for i, multiply by 12).

Comment

Other factors can also affect the lender's yield, e.g., prepayment penalty, participation, etc.

EXAMPLE 11: EXTRACTING AN R_E FROM A SALE

A property sold for \$750,000 with an expected NOI of \$73,500. The buyer assumed a mortgage of \$459,631 with monthly payments of \$4,232.70. A cash equivalency adjustment of -\$7,000 is appropriate. What R_E is reflected by this sale?

Solution

$$
\begin{aligned}
I_E &= NOI - I_M \\
&= \$73{,}500 - 12(\$4{,}232.70) \\
&= \$22{,}708
\end{aligned}
$$

$$
\begin{aligned}
V_E &= V_O - V_M \\
&= \$750{,}000 - \$459{,}631 \\
&= \$290{,}369
\end{aligned}
$$

$$
\begin{aligned}
\text{Therefore } R_E &= I_E / V_E \\
&= \$22{,}708/\$290{,}369 \\
&= 0.0782 \text{ or } 7.82\%.
\end{aligned}
$$

Alternative Solution

$R_M = I_M/V_M = 12(\$4{,}232.70)/\$459{,}631 = 0.1105$, $R_O = NOI/V_O = \$73{,}500/\$750{,}000 = 0.0980$, and $M = \$459{,}631/\$750{,}000 = 0.6128$. Thus, by the band-of-investment technique:

Mortgage	0.6128 x 0.1105	=	0.0677
Equity	0.3872 x R_E	=	$0.3872R_E$
	R_O	=	0.0980
Therefore:	$0.0677 + 0.3872R_E$	=	0.0980
	$0.3872R_E$	=	0.0303
	R_E	=	0.0783, or 7.83%

Comment

The $750,000 used above should *not* have been adjusted for cash equivalency because the amount invested (equity and lender) is actually $750,000 ($290,369 + $459,631).

EXAMPLE 12: EXTRACTING Y_E FROM A SALE

A property sold for $900,000 with 35% down and the balance secured by a loan bearing interest at 9% over a term of 20 years with monthly payments. The buyer expects NOIs to be level at $85,000 for five years due to a lease. At the end of five years the tenant is expected to buy the property for $990,000. What equity yield rate (Y_E) can be extracted from this sale?

Solution

The cash flows for the property, mortgage, and equity are as follows:

Year	Property	Mortgage	Equity
0	-900,000	-585,000	-315,000
1	85,000	63,161	21,839
2	85,000	63,161	21,839
3	85,000	63,161	21,839
4	85,000	63,161	21,839
5	85,000	63,161	21,839
5	990,000	518,936	471,064

Using a calculator or computer, the IRR or Y_E for the equity column is 14.37%.

Comment

The $900,000 used above should *not* have been adjusted for cash equivalency.

EXAMPLE 13: EXTRACTING Y_{LF} FROM A SALE

The leased fee interest in a small shopping center sold for $750,000. Based on existing leases, the net rent for years 1 through 7 is expected to be $60,000, $60,000, $63,000, $65,000, $65,000, $65,000, and $70,000 respectively. At the end of Year 7 the leases will expire and the property is expected to be worth $900,000. What leased fee yield rate (Y_{LF}) can be extracted from this sale?

Solution

The cash flows associated with the leased fee interest are as follows:

Year	Cash Flow
0	-750,000
1	60,000
2	60,000
3	63,000
4	65,000
5	65,000
6	65,000
7	70,000
7	900,000

Using a calculator or computer, the IRR of these cash flows is determined to be 10.53%, the Y_{LF} for the sale.

Comment

The $750,000 should be a cash equivalent selling price.

EXAMPLE 14: ESTIMATING Y_{LF} AND Y_{LH} USING $Y_{LF} < Y_O < Y_{LH}$

The fee simple value of a property is estimated at $500,000 with a first year NOI of $45,000. NOI and value are expected to increase at a compound rate of 3.5% per year for the foreseeable future. A tenant is under contract to pay $40,000 (net) per year for the next three years. What is the probable magnitude of Y_{LH}?

Solution

This solution uses the relationships $Y_{LF} < Y_O < Y_{LH}$ and $Y_O = R_O + CR$. From the above data, $R_O = \$45,000/\$500,000 = 0.09$. $Y_O = R_O + CR = 0.090 + 0.035 = 0.125$, or 12.5%. Y_{LF}, therefore, should be less than 12.5% unless something in the marketplace clearly dictates otherwise. The difference would be a function of the risk involved. Y_{LH}, of course, would be expected to be greater than 12.5%. Note that based on the given information, only the upper limit of Y_{LF} and the lower limit of Y_{LH} can be established.

EXAMPLE 15: ESTIMATING Y_{SAND} AND Y_{SLH}

Bowen leased a parcel of vacant land to Mobley for 15 years for $5,000 per year net. After one year, Mobley subleased the parcel to Gordon for 14 years for $7,000 per year net. Gordon built a small building on the site and is using it for a used car lot. The market rent for the improved property is $12,500 per year net. The value of the property in 14 years is expected to be approximately $135,000. As improved, the fee simple value of the property has been estimated at $125,000. Market rent of the fee simple estate is expected to increase slightly over the next 14 years. If the leased fee discount rate (Y_{LF}) is market supported at 9%, what are the expected discount rates for the sandwich position (Mobley) and the subleasehold position (Gordon)?

Solution

$$\begin{aligned} R_O &= I_O/V_O \\ &= \$12{,}500/\$125{,}000 \\ &= 0.10 \end{aligned}$$

CR = 0.0055 (calculator solution with n = 14, PV = -125,000, FV = 135,000, solve for i). Thus, $Y_O = R_O + CR = 0.1055$, or 10.55%. This supports the Y_{LF} of 9% according to $Y_{LF} < Y_O < Y_{LH}$.

The value of the leased fee estate (V_{LF}) = $79,329 (calculator solution with n = 14, i = 9%, PMT = 5,000, FV = 135,000, solve for PV). Therefore the value of the combined leaseholds (Mobley and Gordon) = $45,671 ($125,000 - $79,329). This assumes the whole is equal to the sum of the parts which may not always be true.

The implied discount rate for the combined leasehold interest (Y_{CLH}) = 13.70% (calculator solution with n = 14, PV = -45,671, PMT = 7,500, solve for i).

If combined, the risk rate for Mobley and Gordon is 13.70% and if Mobley's position has a lower risk than Gordon's, then Mobley's risk rate (the sandwich position) must be less than 13.70%. On the other hand, Mobley's position has more risk than Bowen's at 9%. The risk rate (discount rate, or Y_{SAND}) for the sandwich position (Mobley), therefore, must be between 9% and 13.7%.

Example 16: Extracting a Y_{INC} from a Sale

A leased fee interest was purchased for $400,000. The existing lease had eight years left with a net rent of $30,000 per year. The tenant has no options to renew or purchase. In eight years the property is expected to have a market value (fee simple) of $650,000. Because of the tenant's outstanding credit rating, it is reasonable to conclude that the purchaser of the leased fee interest used two discount rates, one for income and one for the reversion, to make the decision to pay $400,000.

If the market discount rate for the reversion (Y_{REV}) is 14%, what discount rate for the income (Y_{INC}) can be extracted from this sale?

Solution

The present value of the reversion = $227,863 (calculator solution with n = 8, i = 14, FV = 650,000, solve for PV).

The $400,000 paid for the leased fee interest can thus be divided into $227,863 for the reversion and $172,137 for the rent payments. The implied discount rate for the rent payments (Y_{INC}) = 8.04% (calculator solution with n = 8, PV = -172,137, PMT = 30,000, solve for i).

Comment

If a single rate were extracted from this sale it would be 12.49% (calculator solution with n = 8, PV = -400,000, PMT = 30,000, FV = 650,000, solve for i). Whether one rate or two rates are used to value a property of this type, the value estimate should not be different. It should also be noted that a Y_{REV} could be extracted in a similar manner if Y_{INC} were known.

PART FOUR

Additional Extraction Techniques

TWO-VARIABLE EXTRACTION TECHNIQUE

Most appraisers extract rates and ratios from market evidence using a single variable which results in a unique answer. For example:

> A property sold for $425,000 with an $80,000 downpayment and the balance in the form of a purchase-money mortgage taken back by the seller. What loan-to-value ratio can be extracted from this sale?

The solution can be found by solving an equation with a single unknown, M, as follows:

$$\begin{aligned} M &= V_M/V_O \\ &= (\$425{,}000 - \$80{,}000)/\$425{,}000 \\ &= \$345{,}000/\$425{,}000 \\ &= 0.8118, \text{ or } 81.18\% \end{aligned}$$

Since about 1980, professional appraisal courses have exposed appraisers to a two-variable extraction technique, which opens the door to a new level of analysis of sales. Mathematically the concept is not new at all and anyone who has taken a first-year algebra course is already familiar with the technique.

The traditional extraction technique, illustrated above, always solves for a single, unique answer. Algebraically, this involves an equation with only one unknown, e.g., $2x + 3 = 11$. Only one value of x will satisfy or solve this equation. The correct answer, of course, is 4.

In the two-variable extraction technique, the equation to be solved has two unknowns, e.g., $x + y = 12$. This equation does not have a unique solution but, rather, an infinite number of solutions in the form of related pairs, some of which are illustrated below:

x	y
6	6
20	-8
1	11
8	3
0.5	11.5
-3	15

Graphically, these infinite solutions would form a line in which every point on the line would be a solution and every point not on the line would ***not*** be a solution.

The following two examples demonstrate use of the two-variable extraction technique as it applies to two yield capitalization techniques: $R = Y - \Delta \times a$ and Ellwood.

Example A: Extracting a Y_O from a Sale — Non-unique Results

A property sold for $300,000 with an expected net operating income of $36,000 during the first year of ownership. The buyer indicated expected income and value to increase at the same constant ratio over the next five years. What property yield rate (Y_O) can be extracted?

Income and value are changing at a constant ratio, therefore, $R_O = Y_O - CR$ is the proper relationship. $R_O = 12\%$. Y_O and CR are two unknowns in the formula. By selecting a range of CRs that begin too small and end up too large, we can be assured of being in the range of "market expectations." Thus, if the appropriate range of CRs is from -2% to 4%, and each of these CRs is substituted into the formula, $R_O = Y_O - CR$, and we solve for Y_O, we have:

CR	Y_O
-2%	10%
-1%	11%
0%	12%
1%	13%
2%	14%
3%	15%
4%	16%

Any extracted pair above (or fractions in between) has market support for use in a yield capitalization analysis. If the property being appraised is comparable to this sale and if discounted cash flow analysis is the appropriate technique, a forecast of a 2% growth in both NOI and value would require a 14% discount rate (Y_O). Another appraiser, appraising the same property, might forecast a 3% growth rate and properly use a 15% discount rate. Both appraisers would have market support for their conclusions and both would arrive at the same value estimate, assuming they agreed on the first year's NOI.

Comment

The use of $R_O = Y_O - CR$ implies the same compound rate of change for both income and value. It also implies a terminal capitalization rate (R_N) equal to R_O. If R_N is expected to be greater than R_O, the technique discussed in Example C could be used in the extraction process.

EXAMPLE B: EXTRACTING Y_E FROM A SALE — NON-UNIQUE RESULTS

A property sold for $1,200,000 with 30% down and the balance secured by a loan bearing interest at 10% over a term of 25 years. Payments are to be made monthly. According to the buyer, NOI is expected to be $114,000 during the first year of ownership. The projection period is five years. If changes in income and value are expected to be equal and behave according to the Ellwood J factor premise, calculate the pairs of Y_E and $\Delta_{O=I}$ that are reflected by this transaction.

The formula to be used is

$$R_O = [Y_E - M(Y_E + P \times 1/S_{\overline{n}|} - R_M) - \Delta_O \times 1/S_{\overline{n}|}]/(1 + \Delta_I \times J)$$

where P = the percentage of the loan paid off

$1/S_{\overline{n}|}$ = is the sinking fund factor at Y_E and

J = is the Ellwood J factor

all calculated over five years.

A range of Y_Es should be selected that begins too low and ends too high so that the probable Y_E is clearly included. For the low end 10% was selected because it is the interest rate for the loan (recall $Y_M < Y_O < Y_E$), and 24% is selected for the high end (unless the seller was uninformed). Repeated substitutions (one for each Y_E) result in the following table:

Y_E	$\Delta_{O=I}$
10%	2.2%
12%	5.3%
14%	8.7%
16%	12.3%
18%	16.1%
20%	20.2%
22%	24.6%
24%	29.3%

This table shows some pairs of Y_E and $\Delta_{O=I}$ that can be supported by this sale. An appraiser would have market support for forecasting a 20% change in income and value and a 20% discount rate for the equity position. On the other hand, a forecast of $\Delta_{O=I}$ of 25% paired with a Y_E of 16% would be completely contrary to this transaction.

Comment

Since $\Delta_O = \Delta_I$, the terminal capitalization rate (R_N) is assumed to be equal to R_O. If this assumption were not reasonable, and R_N is expected to be greater than R_O, the formula could easily be modified by letting Δ_O be some fractional value of Δ_I, e.g., $\Delta_O = 0.95\Delta_I$.

EXPANSION OF THE RELATIONSHIP Y = R + CR

$Y = R + CR$ is a variation of the model $R = Y - \Delta \times a$ as it applies to a constant-ratio change in income over a projection period. Implicit in this relationship is the requirement that both income and value are changing at the same compound rate (CR). Also implicit, therefore, is the fact that the terminal capitalization rate (R_N) is exactly the same as the "going in" capitalization rate (R_O). For most properties and in most markets, R_N is expected to be higher than R_O for the reasons outlined in the discussion of R_N (see page 28).

The following list of cash flows illustrates the concepts reflected in the relationship $Y_O = R_O + CR_{I=O}$:

Year	Cash flow	
0	-100,000	
1	10,000	
2	10,400	
3	10,816	
4	11,249	
5	11,699	+ 121,670
6	12,167	

The line between years 5 and 6 denotes a five-year analysis with the number below the line ($12,167) being used to determine the reversion ($121,670). An analysis of the cash flows will reveal an R_O and an R_N of 10% and a compound rate of change of 4% for both income and value. In addition, the internal rate of return is exactly 14%. Thus,

$$\begin{aligned} Y &= R + CR \\ &= 10\% + 4\% \\ &= 14\% \end{aligned}$$

If the terminal capitalization rate (R_N) were 0.5% higher, or 10.5%, the only number that would change is the reversion of $115,876 ($12,167/0.105). The resultant internal rate of return for the whole property (Y_O) would then become 13.17%, which is less than the 14% above.

Another useful relationship is thus derived. If R_N is expected to be greater than R_O, a formula for estimating a property discount rate is as follows:

$$Y_O < R_O + CR_I$$

where CR_I is the compound rate of change in income only.

How much "less than" the sum of R_O and CR the resultant Y_O will be is a function of the length of the projection period and the incremental difference between R_N and R_O. It can be calculated by solving a relatively complicated formula or by creating a series of cash flows using the appropriate R_O, CR_I, and an R_N, then solving for the internal rate of return (IRR) and subtracting this IRR from the sum of R_O and CR_I. This process is illustrated in Example C.

EXAMPLE C: CALCULATING THE INCREMENTAL DIFFERENCE BETWEEN $R_O + CR_I$ AND $R_O + CR_{I-O}$

If the overall capitalization rate (R_O) for a property is supported at 9.5%, the compound rate of change in income (CR_I) is expected to be 3%, and the terminal capitalization rate (R_N) should be 0.5% higher than R_O in seven years, how much less than 12.5% should the proper discount rate be?

To solve this problem create any simple set of cash flows that are consistent with the above data. For example, if the first year's cash flow were $100, the following cash flows would be apparent:

Year	Cash flow	Calculation
0	1,052.63	100/0.095
1	100.00	Assumed above
2	103.00	100 x 1.03
3	106.09	$100 \times (1.03)^2$
4	109.27	$100 \times (1.03)^3$
5	112.55	$100 \times (1.03)^4$
6	115.93	$100 \times (1.03)^5$
7	119.41	$100 \times (1.03)^6$
7	1,229.87	$100 \times (1.03)^7/0.10$

Using a calculator or computer, the IRR (and also the appropriate discount rate) is 11.93%. The incremental difference, therefore, is 0.57% (12.5% - 11.93%).

EXPANSION OF THE PROPERTY MODEL USING STABILIZED INCOME

The property model $R = Y - \Delta \times a$, as it has been discussed in appraisal curricula, has been limited to three income patterns: level, straight-line change, and exponential change. With the use of an income stabilization technique, however, any series of income that can be forecast can be valued using the level income version of the relationship $R = Y - \Delta \times SFF$.

Income stabilization, as used in this discussion, means creating an ordinary level annuity that is equivalent (has the same present value at a given discount rate) to the forecast incomes for the property being appraised.

EXAMPLE D: USING R = Y – Δ X A TO VALUE A PROPERTY WITH NONPATTERNED INCOME

A property is expected to have incomes of $10,000, $9,500, $9,500, $10,500, and $11,000 over the next five years. In addition, the value of the property is expected to increase by 10%. What is the value of the property if the appropriate discount rate is 11%?

The first step is to stabilize the income as follows:

The present value of the incomes above discounted at 11% is 37,110 (calculator with i = 11, CF_1 = 10,000, CF_2 = 9,500, CF_3 = 9,500, CF_4 = 10,500, CF_5 = 11,000, solve for NPV)

The equivalent ordinary level annuity is $10,041 (calculator with n = 5, i = 11, PV = 37,110, solve for PMT).

The second step is to develop an R_O using the level-income version of the property model:

$$\begin{aligned} R_O &= Y_O - \Delta_O \times 1/S_{\overline{n}|} \\ &= 0.11 - (0.10)(0.1606) \\ &= 0.0939 \end{aligned}$$

The last step is to use the IRV formula to solve the problem:

$$\begin{aligned} V_O &= I_O/R_O \\ &= \$10,041/0.0939 \\ &= \$106,933 \end{aligned}$$

Proof:

Based on the above answer, the cash flows can be calculated:

Year	Cash flow
0	-106,933
1	10,000
2	9,500
3	9,500
4	10,500
5	11,000
5	117,572

Using a calculator or computer, the IRR, or Y_O, is 11%.

Since virtually any series of cash flows can be stabilized into an ordinary level annuity, the use of the property model is virtually unlimited. The major benefit illustrated here is that because the reversion is a function of the value and the value is a function of the reversion, other techniques, while possible, would require the use of algebra or trial and error.

EXPANSION OF THE ELLWOOD FORMULA USING STABILIZED INCOME

The Ellwood formula,

$$R_O = \frac{Y_E - M(Y_E + P \times 1/S_{\overline{n}|} - R_M) - \Delta_O \times 1/S_{\overline{n}|}}{\text{income stabilization factor}}$$

as it has been discussed in appraisal curricula has been limited to four income patterns: level, straight-line J factor, Ellwood J factor, and exponential change. With the use of an income stabilization technique, however, any series of incomes that can be forecast can be valued using the level income version of the relationship $R_O = [Y_E - M(Y_E + P \times 1/S_{\overline{n}|} - R_M) - \Delta_O \times 1/S_{\overline{n}|}]$.

Stabilization here means the same as in the previous discussion except the discount rate is Y_E.

EXAMPLE E: USING THE ELLWOOD FORMULA TO VALUE A PROPERTY WITH NONPATTERNED INCOME

A property is expected to have incomes of $10,000, $9,500, $9,500, $10,500, and $11,000 over the next five years. In addition, the value of the property is expected to increase by 10%. If a 70% loan at 8.5% interest with monthly payments over 20 years is available, what is the value of the property if the appropriate equity yield rate is 16%?

The first step is to stabilize the income as follows:

The present value of the incomes above discounted at 16% is \$32,803 (calculator with i = 16, CF_1 = 10,000, CF_2 = 9,500, CF_3 = 9,500, CF_4 = 10,500, CF_5 = 11,000, solve for NPV)

The equivalent ordinary level annuity is \$10,018 (calculator with n = 5, i = 16, PV = 32,803, solve for PMT).

The second step is to develop an R_O using the level income version of the Ellwood model:

$$R_O = [Y_E - M(Y_E + P \times 1/S_{\overline{n}|} - R_M) - \Delta_O \times 1/S_{\overline{n}|}]$$
$$= [0.16 - 0.70(0.16 + 0.1187 \times 0.1454 - 0.1041) - 0.10 \times 0.1454]$$
$$= 0.0942$$

The last step is to use the IRV formula to solve the problem:

$$V_O = I_O/R_O$$
$$= 10{,}018/0.0942$$
$$= \$106{,}348$$

Proof:

Based on the above answer, the cash flows can be calculated:

Year	Property	Mortgage	Equity
0	-106,348	-74,444	-31,904
1	10,000	7,753	2,247
2	9,500	7,753	1,747
3	9,500	7,753	1,747
4	10,500	7,753	2,747
5	11,000	7,753	3,247
5	116,983	65,605	51,378

Using a calculator or computer, the IRR or Y_E for the equity column is 16%.

Since virtually any series of cash flows can be stabilized into an ordinary level annuity, the use of the Ellwood formula is virtually unlimited. The major benefit illustrated here is that because the reversion is a function of the value and the value is a function of the reversion, and the loan is a function of value and the value is a function of the loan, other techniques, while possible, would require the use of algebra or trial and error.